VISIONS OF NEW BEING

To Rynette,
In gratitude for
your vocation of
loving and educating
children!
Robin
May 23, 2014

VISIONS of NEW BEING

Meditations & Poems

ROBIN IZER

TERRA FIRMA BOOKS
Colorado Springs, Colorado

robinizer@q.com

Published by Terra Firma Books
2166 Giltshire Drive
Colorado Springs, CO 80905

Printed in the United States of America.

ISBN: 978-0-615-95454-7

Library of Congress Control Number: 2014932411

Cover Photo: Charles Coon with technical enhancement by Nicholas Baranek

Terra Firma Books Logo Design:
Nicholas Baranek

DEDICATION

This book is dedicated to

All Beings who

in times past, present, and future

work patiently to preserve and restore

Earth's living systems and vitality.

ꝏ

May our work prosper.

May our work be blessed.

May All Beings and Earth flourish

abundantly.

A portion of the sales of this book will go to support the critical work of one of these three non-profit organizations: the Natural Resources Defense Council, 350.org, or Earth Guardians: Youth for Global Sustainability.

CONTENTS

INTRODUCTION

ART

There is something sacred
about the art.

There is something mysterious
about the heart.

There is always someone
musing in the dark.

Sacred is the mysterious heart
of the art.

The essence that binds together this collection of meditations and poems is the light of liberation, which lies at the heart of being present, right here, right now, in this moment. This state of being—presence—asks that we experience whatever presents itself, without undue personalizing, without the separating wedge of judgment. Being present also entails simply showing up as a responsive, consciously awake human being, called forth at any given time or place to bring into play the transcendent energies we can choose to root into and grow out from. In Buddhism these transcendent energies are named the four divine dwellings: loving-kindness, compassion, sympathetic joy, and equanimity. The practice is to allow these four rich soils to generate the foundation from which we live and move and have our being.

As a poet, I would add a fifth divine dwelling, creative imagination. We wake to joy and to the co-creative endeavors of the transformative arts, sustainable living, and justice for all beings who share this Earth as home. What a daily discipline and practice of patience these evolving, transformative processes command! What auspicious encounters and revelations can and do unfold!

Poetry is a transformative process. Receiving and composing poetry has been a major source of healing medicine for me. Some of the poems in this book have flashed through my gut, through my imagination, and through my hands onto paper, seemingly as messages or teachings from another dimension. I have often felt that a poem was received and dictated from beyond rather than created by me. These poems have welled up and spilled over, pouring into and through me the wisdom I most needed to hear at the time—words and phrases to meditate upon, to absorb into my own heart-of-hearts. This creative exchange has fed me with courage and continual insight. Over decades, it has helped free me.

The question of whether these poems have ultimately been penned from beyond the veil, from the collective-creative unconscious, or from within my own higher self is a question I leave open. Increasingly, it appears to me that there is truly no separation between these multiple realms of being, just a spectrum or a web of constantly sparking interactions. I sometimes imagine our Universe to be a meta-neuro-network within which each of us is synaptically enmeshed. The creative impulses are constantly flowing through space, sparking in and out, rendering us all more alive and awake, if only we open to them.

Among the fruits I have harvested from this engagement with the enlivening power of words, chant, and spirit-inspired poetry is my own spiritual ripening. I am gradually letting go of anger and resentments. I am continuing to walk the path towards a more balanced, forgiving, and joy-filled life. Let me be clear. I am not undergoing this transformation in any linear or easy progression but with effort, commitment, and the loving help of friends and teachers of tenderness and insight along the way.

Through my exposure to the teachings of the Buddha and those of his trustworthy practitioners over the past 2,500 years, I continue to be fundamentally shaken open by the insights of this wise legacy that penetrate so deeply into the nature of the human psyche and the nature of reality.

The words of Jack Kornfield, Pema Chödrön, Lama Surya Das, Nicole Grace, the Dalai Lama, Joko Beck, Thich Nhat Hahn, Sharon Salzberg, Adyashanti, Chögyam Trungpa, Dipa Ma, Dilgo Khyentse, Dzogchen Ponlop, among others, have opened up endless gates into freedom and wisdom, as have the ancient texts that have carried the Buddha's path and teachings into the present. I must also add to this list of teachers Ram Dass and his beloved guru, Neem Karoli Baba. *Journey of Awakening* by Ram Dass was my first book of formal meditation instruction and remains a favorite still.

My root sangha, Rocky Mountain Insight (RMI), and other Buddhist groups in the Pikes Peak region, give me space, silence, and community to integrate these teachings into the living fabric of my everyday interactions and relationships. I am especially indebted to the teachers and practice leaders at RMI for their devotion to holding space for our weekly sits—and especially to our founder, Lucinda Green, for manifesting and nurturing her vision for Rocky Mountain Insight.

In addition to Buddhism, the transcendent energies and

wisdom of other major spiritual traditions have guided my transformative process. I have been greatly emboldened by the fierce and gentle love of the Goddess in all her cross-cultural embodiments; the winged words of Sufi poets Rumi and Hafiz; the passionate voices of so many female mystics and poets (Rabia, Hildegard of Bingen, Denise Levertov, Mary Oliver, Jane Hirshfield, to name but a few); the Zen wit and wisdom of Basho and Issa; the passion for justice and forgiveness of Jesus of Nazareth; as well as the infinite compassion of the Buddha. All are endless wells of learning and illumination.

I hasten to add that I make no claim to being an enlightened being. Self-deception, emotional reactivity, and sheer sloth are perils I contend with while walking my own evolving path. I have, however, experienced periods of resting in the mystery of boundless silence and fusing with the divine oneness of all being. I strongly believe these dimensions are the natural birthright of all human beings, seekers or not.

I also believe that experiencing these states of glorious being is no guarantee of enlightened behavior in everyday life. Think of all those beautiful lamas and gurus gone astray after their immersion into materialist American culture! This is where daily practice, discernment, integration, and devotion to truth and to the well-being of all sentient beings come into play. The guidelines and teachings of a spiritual tradition as well as trustworthy teachers and spiritual friends are essential. Make no mistake, the seductions of ego are ever-present, and human beings who feel they needn't be vigilant on a daily basis are karmically kidding themselves.

Consciously intending to embody the Six Paramitas (Perfections) from the Buddhist perspective—generosity, ethical conduct, patience, joyful effort, mindfulness meditation, and wisdom—is a lifelong, noble, daily practice.

My spiritual journey has been an evolving process of wending my way back to basic sanity, inherent stability, and finally, to joy and gratitude. Gratitude for this unique experience of a human life in this time and this place on planet Earth. Decades ago, I was a vulnerable, super-sensitive, frightened child, struggling with the dramas of a family system enmeshed in a cobweb of addictive, unconscious behaviors. The confusion and emotional wounding I experienced are all too common in modern American family life. Several of the spiritual teachers I most esteem—Jack Kornfield, Sharon Salzberg, and Dipa Ma—came through deep personal suffering into the light of liberation. Out of necessity, I too followed a path of spiritual seeking and practice.

That I have lived long enough to sample but a taste of the fruits of liberation is a blessing I give thanks for daily. For the resolution of some of my family's causes of suffering, I give joy. For the teachers, the teachings, and the dedicated community of practitioners, my gratitude is endless.

ঌ৩

The meditations and poems in this volume are divided into four sections: Seeing, Practice, Loving, and Earth.

- Poems in the *Seeing* section are mainly records of some of the meditative and visionary experiences I've had while sitting formal meditation, contemplating, dreaming, or simply being open to the wonder of this incredible, intimate journey of living.
- The second group of poems, *Practice*, speaks to the need to integrate these insight experiences into everyday life

interactions and into our relationships with all sentient beings—something I refer to as the ongoing practice of bringing to fruition the seeds of meditative experiences and insights.

- *Loving* includes many of the poems I've written to or about members of my own family and dear friends, as well as the greater family of all our relations.

- And finally, the *Earth* poems celebrate our magical, magnificent Earth and Universe, and all the myriad creatures we are blessed to encounter daily, if we have but eyes to see—birds, flowers, trees, deer, moon, sun, stars, and light itself.

Many of these poems could fit comfortably into any one of these baskets. For example, walking with nature often morphs into a visionary experience, and family interactions can at the same time be a path of practice. But I have been moved to place them where I felt intuitively they wanted to go.

My sincere wish is that these poems may lighten your journey and bring joy and courage to your own life, as they have lightened mine. May you be nourished. May you be filled with gratitude and light. May All be Well!

In gratitude,
Robin Izer
March 2014
Colorado Springs, Colorado

Part One

SEEING

EYES WIDE SHUT OPENED

I fell into a silence
so deep
it was not so much
a falling
as
dissolving
into silence
so radically
there was
nothing
left of me
but watching

not with eyes
not with mind
just watching

watching
silence being aware
of itself
still & infinite
profoundly quiet
like being suspended
weightlessly
within the heart

of the universe
without sound or
sensation

just resting
just being
within this pool
of sacred
silence

and then
after who can tell
how long
the aperture widened
and
I could again
hear sounds
coughing
bodies shifting
smells resumed
while this formal
meditation session
ended

but that center
of stillness
of numinous silence
held that day
anchored
in expanded awakeness
in an elemental beingness

I’d never
disappeared into before
so utterly
so spontaneously
so effortlessly

of this experience
I can say only
I felt held
curious &
home

after time’s passing
this gift
remains a treasure
of refreshment
even still

ONE-POINTED SHELL MIND

I take this shell

in my fingers

to watch

to listen to

with mind's eye.

I breathe &

look.

As nakedly as possible

I simply look.

Without judgment

without chatter of

cascading thought

breath

eye

mind &

shell

intersect at the point

of stillness

dissolve into

emptiness

where for no-time

no-self rests in

boundless space.

SPIRAL

Becoming
is a
spiral
of encounters
with the false self

twining round
greeting
the ever-emerging
true self

in this journey
ever-evolving

learning to see
through the eyes
of the heart

illuminating
the one true nature
of all things

as they simply
are.

UNDERSTANDING WHICH PASSES BEYOND ALL KNOWLEDGE

There was nothing unusual about the day.
In fact, it was dreary—one of those thickly
over-cast New England mornings where
the sky is a solid cake of low-hovering cloud.

The god-forsaken 1950s style coffee shop
where I sat was a vacant hangar of space.
I felt like an Edward Hopper cipher glowing
in the eerie florescent lighting. The cracking
formica tabletop was grey-brown as were the
floor, the walls, the ceiling, and the air in between.

I sat aimlessly waiting for the DMV to open so
I could renew my driver's license. While I stirred
my cup of watery grey-brown coffee—it tasted
like days-old dishwater—I looked down at my
hand holding the chipped white coffee cup and
suddenly, I watched as my fingers disappeared.

My wrist dissolved into the grey-brown table, my
legs melted into the grey-brown chair. I looked
out the window, or perhaps I should say I some-
how floated out the window and my sense of who
I was that morning fused with the scene at that
very crossroads in Watertown Square. It melded
with the metal cars, the people walking quickly by,

the stone bridge, the cement buildings, the stray winter birds foraging for some speck of food, and with the whole of the air that penetrated and encircled everything I could see. All became clear, transparent, calm, still—just as it was.

The fact that I did not find this episode strange in the least still haunts me as I write of this phenomenal occurrence just now. While waiting for the DMV to open some 25 years ago in a greasy grey coffee house, the porous envelope of my animal body instantaneously gave way as my consciousness fused into all matter about me. But I was a busy woman with a new baby at home and a job to get to as soon as this errand was accomplished, and the magnitude of this day slipped inside me as the sun dropped below the horizon each day.

I realized, only slowly, sometime after (although I was aware then of writings which described such things) that I'd been gifted with a bodily immersion into an ancient, sacred understanding which speaks ecstatically that not only shall all things be well, all things are inextricably one as well.

INSIGHT

—for Lucinda Green

I acknowledge
the mysteries beyond
this Earth
I cannot fathom
but sense are
brilliantly present
when
stars, moons & planets
unrobe at night.
I bow
to the powers
I cannot grasp
in my hands
but intuit through
the fingertips of my heart.
I honor
all things
miniscule and exponential
spinning & sprinting
through space
on threads
of light.
May I & all beings
aspire to
vibrate harmoniously
within this
luminous web.

May I & all beings
awaken
within this
infinite field
to openness
to inquiry
to apprehend
our boundless journey
with inner
sight.

KAIROS

Moments of time
sweet untrained gifts of light
where endless time breaks through.

Moments of time
calling from beyond the veil
where distance
between myself and the unlimited
is wholly telescoped.

Moments of time
where time is suspended,
immersed in experience
utterly, I am only
in being, not time.

Moments of time
I know my intimate connection
to stars, to beasts,
to deity is real,
not longing.

Moments of time
incalculable pure delight
like unabashed song
winging out into the universe
and streaming back ignited.

MOUNTAIN QUESTIONS WITH TAOS MOUNTAIN IN MIND

> "What we are is revealed, ultimately,
> by the questions we ask, rather than
> by the answers we find."
>
> —Deena Metzger

How do you
take the mountain
inside you?

How do you
bear all that
mass with such
lightness of being?

How do you
dwell in such
deep silence
that speaks eons
of digested wisdom?

When does
the triangle
embrace the circle
only to disappear
into the endless
horizon?

DWELLING PLACE

I have been there
in the wind sweeping the seas.

I have been there at dusk
in the cricket's chirping.

I have been there
in the rose, in the dew
at dawn.

I have been there
in the spring, in the sweet
green smell of
lilies of the valley.

I have been there
in the fall, in the crackling smoke
of orange-red leaves.

I have been there
in the ice, in the sacred geometry
of each filigreed snowflake.

I have been there
in the sun, in the warming arms
of the blue noon day.

I have been there
in the sky, in the air
in the Earth pushing up thin
seedlings to light.

I have been there
in your joy, in your rejoicing,
in your hopes, at your hearth.

I am there at your
waking, in your sleeping,
in your love and
every desire.

I have been there
calling you by name
caressing your heart.

WHAT AM I?

I am no thing
I am nothing
I am multitudes
I am laundry

I am whatever I am being
this present moment

I am flow
ever changing, ever same

I am all
contradictions
interchanging, resolving
into one

I am rainbow
light, silence
exploding star, void

I am true nature
Awareness
Awareness of Awareness
Witness

I am
Self, Other

Self & Other
Intertwined, hologrammed

Being/Inter-Being
Essence/The 10,000 Things
Paradox of the
Formless transforming into form/
Form transforming into formlessness

Simply Spirit
Vanishing into Mystery

I AM
I AM
I AM

No separation
No Story
Loving whatever is
Canticle of the Spheres

Aware
Awake
Arising

Nothing into
Nothing

One

AFTERNOON NAPPING

I vanish, incrementally

on the vector of sleep

disappearing quietly

into mystery

into vision

into lost, lovely, slumbering

sweet no-time.

BODY FLIGHT

You rise from bed
where you've been
reading, musing for hours
startled to discover
in the mirror
your own fleshy face
and a solid body

startled because
contemplation was
your sole embodiment
for what seemed
like days passing

while your earthly
body drifted out the
window and escaped
to another realm
of refreshment.

SWAN

Ah, how tranquilly
this white-feathered
swan glides
across the
buoyant membrane
of lake water
oblivious to
murkiness below,
mutability above.
Perhaps this
white swan
may simply be
a recent Bodhisattva
beaming innocent
grace & inspiration
knowingly yet modestly
with each understated but
elegant gesture,
with harmonious flow
and pace.

GRACE

More than anything

I want to be the

simple flower

the Buddha held up

during his

speechless discourse

or the

simple smile

on the face

of the one disciple

who realized fully

this silent teaching

of the Buddha

with such

simple grace.

MORNINGS

—for Maria Battista

May all mornings
be blessed
with the rush
of new vistas
opening
into knowledge
as yet
unrecovered—
for visions
unearthed
from the world
of dreams to be
fashioned into
stone, paint or script
the work of our
human hands
mind resting in heart—
for feelings
shared with the
soft fingers of courage
inspiriting
intimacy & healing.

May all mornings
be blessed by
twining the
seeming dualities
into a cloak
of compassion
to lighten
our sufferings.
May we begin again
afresh
with each
new sunrise
to explore ever deeper
the true nature
of our humanness &
to expand the
spaciousness
of our radiant bodies
into light.
With all gentle
unfolding
may this be so!

I DREAMT LAST NIGHT

I dreamt last night
green arms of grass rose up
and overtook the city.
They call this
wilderness sprawl.

I dreamt last night
animals of all kinds
two by two
stole into the cities
and marched the humans
back to secret dens
to rehabilitate them in the
ways of Earth.
They call this
humanitarian aid.

I dreamt last night
the stars and planets
took to heart the sight of
pollution, stench, and chaos
wafting up from Earth
and pledged to send
healing light and
extraterrestrial guidance.
They call this
celestial salvation.

I dreamt last night
the plants, animals, humans
stars and planets all conspired
to fulfill the dream of Earth
and with the swirling energies
of the Universe
they resounded the heavens with
song & dance, mutual growth & joy.
We call this
reign of peace.

JUST BEING

So, just being
and becoming
more being
isn't such a
bad way
of being
in this world
where so much
doing has become
the extinction
of so many
beings
we are never again
to see
waking on this
star-lit Earth.

And so I say
here's to being
just pure plain being
here's to
much more of it
on this
our star-lit
Earth.

DEATH

The last person
I touched
before I died
was my killer—
the knife
ripped my flesh
exploded
my heart—
my eyes pierced his
and with
soft utter surprise
I whispered
I love you
then effortlessly
fell into his arms.

VISION

When I lay down
close my eyes
I see.

In spacious domain
vision appears to me.
Welled-up from
dark chambers of
deep reverie.

When I lay down
close my eyes
I see.

Beauty walks round
spins her yarn
weaves her trees.

When I lay down
close my eyes
I see.

Lapis, turquoise
peacocks and seas.
Orchids, rainbows
sunsets and peace.

When I lay down
close my eyes
I see.

DREAMS, LIKE POEMS

Poems, like dreams
rest briefly in the mind
as skywriting quickly
scrolls then evaporates
from skies.

Celestial communications
breathe manna into bone into flesh.
Awake now. Listen.
Great Soul is speaking.

Here are words
which heal or prick the gut.

Here are sounds
pouring music into the world.

Take this medicine
and live.

SITTING

—for Donna Becker

If I don't make time
to sit

to simply gaze
upon
this sky & mountain vista
in quiet
effortless
reverie

a whole
chunk of my awareness
goes wasting.

Confusion of a splintering sort
descends
all around & within
defeating any clever ploys
to arrest it.

There is but one
antidote
I know
to this wasting illness—

to sit
in perfect
innocent
stillness
and breathe.

To become
centered
in a more
spacious, forgiving
reality
once again.

Part Two

☙ PRACTICE ❧

JOYFUL EFFORT

Making space

making time

for this transformation

for a realignment

    for compassion's sake

from the inside

out.

PRACTICE, PRACTICE, PRACTICE

In all things
at all times
slow down
& just be more

present.

LET THE WAY BE

Let the way

be gentle

like velvet

or the silk of

summer corn tassel.

Let the way

be humourous

brimming with

delight & spontaneity

like the

mirthful surprise

of two-year-olds

exploring their

daily wonders.

Let the way

be one of

ever-expanding

welcome

verified by

the softening

the deepening

of the heart's wisdom—

wisdom rooted

in the womb of

gentleness

humour

forgiveness

and

openness

to more of this.

DIFFERENT QUALITY OF CHANGE

Ah . . .
first time
with budding
awareness
of moving
more gracefully
through the
complex dance
of change—
assessing what is &
what is not
weighing paths
dispassionately
deciding consciously
with the wholeness
of my being intact
rather than
mucking about
confused
split
rushed &
ultimately disappointed.
Taking smaller
mindful steps
to create
a more discerning
conduit

for the infinite
energy of potential
to manifest itself
clearly, cleanly
in its own time
while the true self
welcomes what is
opening up
with grateful heart.

KINDNESS

I strew the path

with lilies of kindness

first towards myself

then all others.

I remember

the way is

beautiful

so much lighter

when I drop

my obsessive

self-circling worries

and simply breathe

into each present step

of the way.

I practice

clear mind open heart

clear mind open heart

re-minding myself

of this teaching

with each outgoing

each incoming

breath.

Each day I strive to

allow the honey

of kindness

its natural flow.

It offers such sweetness

to all beings

every moment

we open in awareness

no matter what.

MEDICINE MUSIC

Listen for your song
let it pour through you
like clear water
falling off steep rock
soaking your inmost being.
If you wait and witness
soon enough you will feel
the rhythm that pulses
your unique beat in time.
Listen deeper.
Listen wisely.
This is the melody
that enchants & softens
the heart—
the music that imprints
the joy of being on
your soul's journey.

DISSOLVING

The way
is not perfect
we are impatient
we are unkind.
Our charge
is to notice
these states
to rest
in these
uncomfortable
places—
simply to
witness
wait & watch
to breathe with it
to breathe into it
breathe it out
as impatience or
unkindness
gradually dissolves.
May you notice
over time
the duration
between
impatience
to dissolving
will narrow.

May your whole
being smile
when you begin
noticing this.
Practice only
quickens this
dissolving resolution.
Gently re-mind
yourself—
practice, practice
wherever you are.

WALK ON

> A student asked a Zen Master,
> "What is absolute truth?" And the
> Zen Master said only, "Walk on!"

If only you waken

to that which

walks beside you

you will never

grow faint

or weary—

for that which

walks beside you

within you, through you

is nothing less

than the infinitely spiraling

energies of the mystery

which ignite

the stars, the universes

the very

substance & fragrance

of all life—

this mystery generates

the love-force to become

embodied

this mystery continues waking

moment by moment

throughout the blooming universes

through every conscious breath

of your very own

spiritbody.

Honor & nourish

the presence

of this mystery

within, without

& walk on.

UPON RISING

Before you rise from bed

take one minute

to breathe into this . . .

Go forth each day

with humble compassion

for both yourself

and all beings

you meet on the journey.

Make loving understanding

your response in all

interchanges.

Be patient with

the small & sometimes

large irritations which will

inevitably cross your path.

Remember to take

time to breathe deeply
from your belly
to replenish your
life force which will
also restore
depth & balance
to your being.
In all things,
Patience
Compassion
Love
and not least, a touch of
Good Humour.
Remember to smile often;
all things are passing
all things are impermanent.
Do not hold onto
what is tight or small.

Root and grow

your being

in what is true, in what

expands and forgives,

in what provides

divine nourishment

to the living soul.

To you, may all be well!

UNCERTAINTY

Living between
two points
where no bridge
yet exists.
Not knowing "for sure"
is so hard
for this human being.
May I aspire
to rest easy
trusting
without reservation
without anxiety
trusting that what
will happen
will happen
will be just as it is
& knowing I will
arrive safely
whatever happens
just as I have
time past time present
time future.
My present learning is
to unconditionally trust—
to trust in only
this certainty
all will be well

all will be well
no matter what
all will be well.
(In truth
there are no points
and no bridges
simply eternal
flow.)

CHOICELESS CHOICE

In the past
internal deliberation
smoldered & stumbled
for what seemed like
a chaotic eternity.
Since practicing mindfulness
more consciously
the way
appears
to resolve
into a lit path
more quickly,
more quietly.
On occasion
feet just seem
to take their own
direction now
walking me.

YOGA CLASS

Tonight

the yoga went inside—

each movement flowing

so much more effortlessly

than before,

a sweeping

meditation-in-motion.

Each movement

mindful & quiet

sinking deep within the body's spirit

and the spirit's body

united—

one vibrating breath of life.

MEDITATION-IN-MOTION

I recollect
the inner voice
of the yogi
who woos me
to meditation-in-motion

"It is completely safe
to let go
it is completely safe
to let go
it is completely safe
to let go

to let go
let go
let go

let completely go."

AWAKE NOW

Each day
new dawn
new adventure

joy of
not knowing

just present
still
awareness.

Fresh light.

SONG

If you sing

keep singing.

The practicing voice

grows stronger

clearer each day

vibrating with light.

OBSTACLES

The way is paved

with obstacles

if we choose

to perceive them

as obstacles

or

we can

experience these

inevitable hurdles

along the way

as high stepping stones

taken slowly

thoughtfully

building muscle

and will

toward a wider

vision of reality.

May we mark

these daily lessons

where we accept

what is

unconditionally

and at the

same time

may we move

out of the way

what needs removing—

embracing

these two

states of

intertwined being

with

equanimity & balance.

ALLELUIA!

Life is really very
simple
once you get the
hang & heft
of it.

Do what needs to be
done, do what's right
in front of you

with attentive devotion
with pleasure
whatever it is!

Be of service
where and when
you can.

And most of all
love your
near & cosmic life
here & now

it passes
all too quickly.

ABIDING

Joy

abides in this moment

doing what needs to be done

with attention

skillfulness

with quiet patience.

Joy

abides in this moment

noticing

the way light

sculpts into being

the ten thousand things

the lily pond

the perfect blossoming

of the blush-pink lotus.

Joy

abides in this moment

when we sit

over a cup of tea

sharing

laughter & those

places in our hearts

with vulnerability

& mirth.

Joy

abides in each moment

we are present

here and now

no matter where we

might be traveling.

MAKING

The poem
writes itself
petal by petal
as the blossom opens.
It gathers itself
and opens outward
fed by the stem
of its own
seed and cells.
Free and fumbling forward
the poem works itself
to shape,
evolves until
a certain instinct
discerns the surprise
of unity—
a ripened apple
beaming light.

WHAT ARE HUMAN BEINGS FOR?

We are here
to pay attention
to be present
to listen

to respond
with compassionate
open hands
open hearts

which humbly ask—
How, if I can
may I help?

NO CONSTANT BUT CHANGE

The way

will take you

if you let it.

Nothing but change

Nothing but flow

Nothing but transformation.

Even in the

driest desert

the yellow cactus flower

blooms then dies

then blooms anew.

LETTING GO INTO LIGHT

Do not clutch
flow
let go &
know the richness
of the Universe
is your own estate.

Take gently
and receive the wealth
of all creation.

You are a child of Light—
your inheritance is divine
and lies beyond
all expectation.

Do not clutch
flow
let go &
accept the knowledge
of your own immortal soul.

Regard that still small voice
wooing your inmost heart
and honour the
wisdom she whispers.

Do not clutch
flow
let go &
leap!

Part Three

☙ LOVING ❧

WEB

The way
is a circuit
of connections
intertwining
plants, animals
humans, stars
& galaxies
into the beyond.
All are kin
all constitute
this web
called home.
When a star
explodes
another dimension
its vibration
shifts energy
in our
backyard.
Weaving this truth
into the fabric
of our daily lives
may all connections
illuminate
our delicate
interdependence

may all connections
perpetuate
the humming
of this infinite
formless form
forever birthing
the 10,000 things
our family
of beings.

LOVE'S MYSTERIES

Who you love

and how you

learn to

love them

is truly a

mysterious thing.

FRIENDS

Like trees

linked arm to arm

at the edge

of a field of red poppies

friends stand with you

through the changing weathers

of life.

WHAT TRUE HUMAN BEINGS WANT

We want the children fed.

We want the children healthy and educated
to joy and usefulness.

We want the violence and wars ended.

We want the noble vegetables, fruits and
grain grown for every body's nourishment.

We want the Earth respected and tenderly
restored, not raped or poisoned or possessed.

We want the women and men of all diverse natures
equal and entitled to the fruits of human
dignity, justice, work, community, and celebration.

We want our Earth to endure and we want it
spun by caring devotion, not possession-power.

We want to grow old to tell the young our stories.

We want love, and more, we need compassion
to transform our world's way from
dominance to mutuality.

We want life to grow and build and become new life.

We want to become what we were created to be—
sisters and brothers sharing Earth's bounty
and tending the creation that is our most
sacred dwelling place.

So be it!

THREE QUESTIONS

—for Paul Burke

How does a
body heal?

How does a
self become
whole?

How does a
being evolve
to help heal
others and
our planet home?

RENEWAL

Standing in the cool room silent,
seeming opposite colours of
life's spectrum,
we touched fingers.

Spanning the separation,
fused the wavelengths.

Clear morning light.

INTIMATE ACCEPTANCE

In your circle
of closest relations
there are inevitably
these innocent
bits of behavior
of the other
which bite like fleas
into your falsely
righteous flesh.
These you must
simply let fall away
into the deep ocean
of acceptance.
These petty stings
that burn with
the fire
of outraged irritation
will extinguish
through mindful
witness
seeing them for
what they truly are—
opportunities to
practice bodhichitta
bodhipatience
in the moment.

Eventually these
bites which once
tossed you
into the abyss
of separation
will transform
into the very acts
which endear
you to the other
now one
with you
in your
awakening heart.

SAGE DANCER

—for Barbara Counts

She dances in the night
nude as a baby
an arthritic old crane
but still
sashaying, prancing
twirling
to the invisible music
beating deep inside her
softly folding flesh.
Late, late into the night
only starlight
only moonlight
accompany
these authentic gestures
of a fierce
free old bird
spinning bright memories
into nests of gold.

BIRTH

In that moment, much
anticipated miracle
I thought,
"Dear God,
I've delivered forth
a fish!"

You whirled out of me
like a flapping red snapper
urgent to gulp air.

I duly recorded,
it was the queerest
sensation my inner
thighs had ever known.
Nearly comical.

Then I looked
down upon your
rushing forth
in humbled awe,
startled to find
a tiny wet person
all new.

AFTER THE BATH IN THE P.M., GOODNIGHT

—for my daughter, Myka

When I'm rocking you I think
how like a little chimpanzee you are
clinging to my breast-fur
all worn out from a hard day's play
in the savannah.

Alas, how I wish we could enjoy
the morrow's absent-minded pleasures
of tree-perching and preening
the little what-nots
from each other's hairs.

But little one, your mommy
grubs for money day in and day out,
just to keep your sparsely-furred flesh
from freezing in winter.

O human toil, animal frolic!
Would that we possessed less brain
more prehensile muscle
to squander the day swinging!

Every now and again
at the office

I see us swooping
branch to blossom
as gay as two old farts
peeling bananas.

My tawny-scrawny little chimp
smelling that musk-downy fragrance,
burrow closer,
rub off some scent
that I might carry you with me
all the day long tomorrow.

FRAGMENT

When you look
into your own
questioning green
eyes

you see your
daughter long
ago

cinnamon tossed
hair

impossibly long
tapered
fingers—

the open
innocent face of
mystery

a flower about to
unfurl.

SENDING PRAYERS

My prayer—

did you feel it

on its wings

swooping into your

heart

warming your

soul-body with its

heat and tears

rinsing your sorrow

to shine you

& buff you

against the new

day's trials?

LUELLA'S GRANDCHILD

I will gather you up
in my arms
of thanksgiving
and curl you
in my love.

I will gather you up
like a bouquet
of fruity freesia
and spread you
round my hearth.

I will gather you up
by squeezing out
your tart juices
my pink sweet pea—
your nectar drips
perfume in my air.

You kindle my fragrance
and my power.
You gather me up
in your gorgeous being
like a radiant
sunflower.

SUNDAY

Sitting in the sun
writing these words.
Watching the sky.
Feeling breeze on my neck.
Scratching the cat's ears.
Talking with Myka about life
justice, loving.

To be.
To grow.
To imagine.
In silence. In harmony.

Range around.
Be a rascal.
Be a cat.

Rest.

THANKSGIVING AFFIRMATION

To settle down
into the power
of this quiet place

to sink into
the grace of silence,
to listen to
the rhythm of blessing
beating beneath
the going and the getting
and the coming back.

I take these moments
on occasion from my
rocking chair
to smile in my heart
nodding yes to how
blessed I am.

How glorious the world is.
How much I love living
and love loving.
How much I want to
feel and taste and touch
and see and love before
I die.

OFFERING OF GRATITUDE FOR THICH NHAT HANH

Written after returning from a retreat with Thay at Compassionate Dharma Cloud Monastery in Morrison, Colorado, on August 28, 2011, with members of Sun Mountain Sangha

Dearest Thay
I bow
to you
to your feet
to your complete
embodiment of
wisdom's grace.
For decades
perhaps lifetimes
your words
your visage
(gentle, noble,
fiercely present)
have lifted me
and so many
guided us
consoled us
inspired us
beyond doubt
& darkness.
Words can play
like shallow reeds

but these seek
only to convey
an ocean of
deep gratitude.
We bow
in humble respect
to the Buddhanature
which emanates
from your being.
We thank you
for your vast kindness
your poetic spirit
your true courage
in times of war &
great suffering
for your infinitely
compassionate path.
May our planet
evolve towards
ever more
harmonious interbeing
& gentle mindfulness
in response
to your presence
& your teachings.
May the ground
always bloom
with sunflowers
wherever you
walk.

Part Four

☙ EARTH ❧

PRESENCE

—Cape Cod, Massachusetts

I see now why
the primitives did it,
why they believed
the finger of the rain god
sent water upon them.

We walked in
the evaporating mist
up the long incline
toward the ocean
where the sparkling
green plane of dune grass
met with the plane
of cold taupe-coloured sand,
met with the plane
of deep-rushing sea.
And all was enveloped
by the globe
of fresh blue air
in which we walked
like the first beings
to witness the miracle
of the Earth's washing
after the first
summer storm.

The Earth, renewed
and cleared as if by
some palpable gesture.
We walked from plane to plane
transformed by the gloria
of warming light, enfolded
in the sweet wet mist
some hand had swirled
out of cloud, as a sign
of presence.

BENET PINES RETREAT

Ponderosa pines
scattered over acres
four feet apart
in every direction,
stand like sacred sentries
guarding all souls
human, animal, divine
who lightly tread here.

The forest moves as one unit
leans to calm breezes
sings to the broad blue sky
praises the snow-capped Peak.

While in my cabin hermitage
I welcome the dawn
from my tiny window,
warming to the memories
and possibilities which will
feed this half-awakened
new day.

COLORADO EVENING

At dusk

after humid rain

        preceded by hail

two deer feed in the

tall green meadow grass,

my footfall startles them.

        They bound up the hill

leaving me sad

to have frightened them,

sorry we cannot

accompany each other

        on this evening's

        short journey.

WEST DENNIS, CAPE COD

It is endlessly reassuring
like a mother
when you return to a piece
of the Earth you love.
It is still there.
Waves, wind, milkweed.

I know this approach to the
sea that thrills my body every time.
Some mornings I wake with
that distant smell
of the salt-sea-sand
in my mind, my eyes, my nose.
The longing is visceral as kinship.

I know I must go
as surely as if grandmother
called to beckon,
"Come, I've missed you, I have
secrets to refresh your dance."

ON THE STOOP, SPRING EVENING

darkness spreads
its inky fingers

a silver planet
silently
spins & shines

lilac perfume lifts
the air

mind pulsates with
10,000 sights & smells

body longs for the
luxury of being
softly held

memory weaves
perceptions
into metaphor
& story

night so quietly
covers all

THE ROUND

day slips into

night, the moon

rises, dreams

blossom, images

well-up into poems

with sun's rising

open sky

clear & blue

PULSE OF THE DAY

Morning bright

with streaming

cotton candy clouds,

green leaves brushing

blue sky—

wild & wide.

This is the day

opening into

choice & change

opening into the feathered

colours of imagination.

This is the given day

to affirm or defile—

holy breathing into holy.

MEDITATION WHILE HIKING

—for Izzy Moreno

From this peace-filled place
resting on a cool granite boulder
I gather
energy from flickering red ladybirds
persistence from this slow-tripping
light shimmering stream.

Opposite me
two ponderosa pine trunks
twine together, reaching up
through the spare forest canopy
into the wonder of open sky.

ONE NIGHT

One late night
at Mabel Dodge's hacienda
I am so drunk
on the moon
hanging out
the tiny window
—a breathing portal into the universe
I fuse
with that giant
luminous eye of black night.
What force
sweeps me so fiercely
like a tiny filing
towards this celestial
magnet?
What lit offering
can I make
to eternity's radiance?
Can I walk
on light?

MOONSET

This impossibly

huge luminous

orb

disappears

bite-by-bite

below

the green line

of foothills—

such deliciously eaten

golden

eye candy!

DUSK SONG

In the setting sun
of Taos
an ancient flute sounds
joyful, mournful spirit tones.

The colour of amber
pours across sagebrush
which runs to the foothills for a mile.
Here, mountains rise like watchful beasts
and late day sun reflects the majesty
of Earth lifting to meet painted sky.

And just when you'd expect
a star to steam across
this vibrating landscape
or the moon to break into white fire,
the flute song fades against the distance,
the colours dim,
and the blue-black night extinguishes all.

SWEET MORNING

Today's sky
is sketched in
wispy nettles
of vapour
while mares' tails
sweep the blue.
Pikes Peak's giant
granite dome
intervenes between
heaven & earth
beaming
the day's wonders
ever changing.
This August morning's
cricket chorus
is fading fast as
the sun thickens
and streams
of squawking tires
ever multiply.
I return to
the day's errands
with eyes
intermittently
on this luminous
sky.

EACH DAY

Each day
I walk
to the water's edge
I lift my arms
attempting to embrace
the infinite light

the light which draws
the ocean's particles
one by one
home.

FIRE ~ EARTH ~ WATER ~ AIR

—for Ann Donovan

You walk out
into the deep sunlight

    steadying your two feet
    into the rich dark Earth

and everything is there
awaiting your heart's embrace—

the shimmering treetops
beaming light

    the mirror of rain
    left by last night's storm
    reflecting the bluest sky

the sheer crisp air

you breathe it all in—

    everything your
    body-mind needs
    to make sweet love.

THE BLESSING OF RAIN

With water
dripping down
the deep bark
of trees,
soaking this Earth
reviving each root

the primal beginnings
of each new thing
awaken

soon to sprout
some variation
of virgin
green.

WONDER WONDER WONDER

—for David Panico

I.

I'm calling to tell you
the birds are singing again,
their mellifluous morning chorus
of song.

It happens every year
in early March
but each new spring
it shatters my heart
over & over again
waking all
that slumbers in these
cold winter veins.

II.

When my eyes
bounce between
this crazy-quilt
of wildflowers
and the twilit
blue sky above

I often think
of flowers as
tiny sparks of
fiery stars
that have fallen
through the coloured
veils of the aurora
borealis to the wild
Earth to bloom.

III.

We have all seen love broken
then restored

seen tiny shoots of green
push up through parched
brown soil and flower.

This growth takes patience
and many seasons
but love does abide
and makes all things new.

ON FINDING A PACKET OF BLUE FLAX SEEDS AMONGST MY SPIRAL JOURNAL NOTEBOOKS

We are poets.

We need to be about
the business
of planting seeds.

Every day!

ACKNOWLEDGMENTS WITH GRATITUDE

With deepest gratitude to the following friends who have generously enriched my creative & spirit life—Maria Battista, Donna Becker, Lylas Becker, Lucy Bell, Shannon & Randy Bowen, Victor Bradford, Tamara & Al Brody, Renée Brabant & Paul Burke, Beth Chorpenning, Diane & Charlie Coon, John Corcoran, Barbara Counts, Constance Davis, Ann & Bob Donovan, Gwen Fox, David Gardiner, the Gault Family, Don Goede, Mary Anne Fay Gunnarson, Lucinda Green, Jane Grosheider, Linda Hodges, Teresa Masterson & John Howe, Patricia Komarow, Eana LaFont, Crystal Bliss & Pete Lardy, Teryl Lundquist, Karla Crescenta & Ann Grant Martin, Jen Mulson, Pat Musick, Kathleen Musser, Marta & Michael O'Laughlin, Jan & Dave Panico, Briane Pinkson, Marie Poole, Jerry Shifrin, Patricia Seator & Richard Skorman, Don Stevens, Ana Golden & John Stone, Rose Trigg, Kat & Bob Tutor, Mark Warshaw, and Sally Whelan.

I also want to honor three community gems that contribute so much to the artistic and intellectual quality of life in the Pikes Peak region—Poor Richard's Bookstore, Manitou Art Center, and the Smokebrush Foundation. My friends and I have engaged in so many inspired and transformative adventures at these welcoming, soul-gathering venues. Thanks to all the devoted staff and the founders who work so creatively to bring such vibrancy into our lives. And an additional shout-out to the brilliant folks at the *Colorado Springs Independent* for keeping us all informed and connected as a community.

With special thanks to members of my long-term book group Tea & Tomes—for sisterhood, stimulating conversation, and support; you girls are the bees knees!

To Paul Burke, for significantly editing and improving the Introduction. To Donna Becker and Maria Battista for reading and offering suggestions on the manuscript in its early stages.

To Donna Becker and Paul Burke for extraordinary achievement in proofreading! Sincere thanks to you both for the precious gifts of your time and talent.

To Ken Guentert of The Publishing Pro, for designing and midwifing this book, and for Charlie Coon's inspired cover photo, I cannot intone *Gracias* enough.

To Nicholas Baranek for creating the lovely lotus logo for Terra Firma Books and for technical assistance on the cover. Thank you for your expertise.

To all the members of Rocky Mountain Insight sangha, profound thanks for sharing the silence, teachings, and community. Without you, my practice would be so much less skillful and compassionate.

To all seekers, poets, and wisdom teachers I have had the privilege to learn from whether in person or through writings, your transformative truth continues to embolden and shape my journey. My reverence is endless.

Warmest gratitude to my family circle—Izers, Schmidts, Bittners, Morenos, and Harmons, near & far—most especially my mother, Jane Izer Schmidt (presently age 91), my father, Thomas Schmidt (presently age 94), my sister, Karen Szachnitowski and her husband Mike Szachnitowski, and to my dear brother Tommy, who died unexpectedly when I was eleven. And also to my dearest uncle, Max Izer (presently age 94).

Finally, a deep and humble bow to those who know me most deeply and keep surrounding me with their love, my dearest daughter, Myka Luella Estes and my dearest husband, Isabel (Izzy) Moreno. The joys and sorrows we've shared are part of the web which make life so bearable and beautiful.

With grace & gratitude for All!

ABOUT THE POET

Robin Izer previously published *Hymns from Earth*, a book of poems and prayers with monotypes by Boston artist Sarah Girard. Robin has supported herself in various roles within the non-profit sector in the arts, education, and human services, including positions at the Denver Art Museum, at Penrose Hospital on a grant from the National Cancer Institute, and at Harvard University. She currently works with special-education middle-school students in Colorado Springs School District 11. Robin earned her B.A. in Art History with a minor in English Literature from the University of Maryland and her M.A. in Pastoral Counseling from Emmanuel College, Boston.

She is particularly consumed with the field of imagination where poetry, spirituality, and inquiry intermingle to create shifts in consciousness and action. Robin teaches occasional workshops on poetry and spirituality at PILLAR Institute for Lifelong Learning and other venues. Her root sangha is Rocky Mountain Insight, founded by Dharma Teacher Lucinda Green.

Robin has birthed one continuously amazing daughter, neuroscientist Myka Estes, and currently resides with her husband, drummer and artist Izzy Moreno, in Colorado Springs, Colorado.

COLOPHON

Visions of New Being

was designed and copy edited by
Kenneth Guentert of the Publishing Pro, LLC
and printed on Neenah Classic Laid paper
in Recycled 100 Natural White.

The typeface is Janson.

The book was printed at Frederic Printing
Aurora, Colorado
in March, 2014.

This edition is limited to
500 copies.